HEART

OF

A

LION

Joshua Lawrence Chamberlain
Scholar/Warrior

HEART
OF
A
LION

by

Jack Bilello
and
Robyn Supraner

To order additional copies of this book, contact:
Xlibris Corporation
1-888-795-4274
www.Xlibris.com
Orders@Xlibris.com
66588

Contents

Chapter I

Young Pioneers

Young pioneers, the Chamberlain family traveled from Massachusetts in a horse-drawn wagon, carrying all of their possessions — and a dark secret. It was 1799 and they were about to settle into their new homestead in Maine.

In 1692, during the tragic Witch Trials in Salem, Massachusetts, Rebecca Chamberlain, a direct ancestor of Joshua Lawrence Chamberlain, was taken from her bed in the middle of the night and burned at the stake as a witch. The wild-eyed man who had pointed his shaking finger at Rebecca, who had hunted her down and condemned her to death, was none other than John Hathorn – a direct ancestor of the great writer, Nathaniel Hawthorne.

For Joshua, born in 1828, well over a century later, that shameful moment and the disgrace it had brought upon the Chamberlain family, still flamed in his heart.

Years passed and, as fate would have it, Nathaniel Hawthorne and Joshua met. Hawthorne, reminded of that wretched time in history, sympathized with the lad and said, "In the depths of every heart, there is a tomb and a dungeon."

*   *   *

Joshua's father, John Chamberlain, was a proud and moral man who stressed the importance of family and self-discipline. "You come from a line of red-blooded and worthy ancestors – seafaring men who built and sailed the longboats, men who fought courageously and with honor in our War for Independence. Like them, you must live by this rule: a sound mind in a sound body. Now, take up your sword, lad! It is time for our duel!"

Joshua took up his weapon, a thirty-five inch dueling sword, grasped it behind the bowl-shaped guard and, addressing his father, took several fast steps forward, and thrust. He enjoyed these mock duels. They were – dare he think it – fun. For, in a Puritan household, fun was a wasteful commodity.

His father, stronger, taller, and more experienced, parried his son's every thrust. Joshua moved swiftly, lunging, withdrawing, taking advantage of his size and speed. At last, laying his hand on Joshua's shoulder, his father said, "Enough for today." He looked with pride at the lad. "I have named you well, my son – Joshua Lawrence, after that great naval hero, James Lawrence, who distinguished himself in our War of 1812. Do you remember what ship he commanded and the famous words that he spoke?"

"I d-d-d-d-o, sir," said Joshua, snapping to attention. "He c-c-c-commanded the f-f-f-f-frigate *Chesapeake* and, though m-m-m-mortally wounded, rallied his m-m-men with the words:

"Tell the-m-m-men to f-f-f-fire faster and not to g-g-g-give up the sh-sh-ship." Today, we remember those f-f-f-famous w-w-words as 'D-d-d-don't give up the sh-sh-ship!'"

There it was again, thought Joshua, the worrisome and hateful stuttering that he would fight so long and hard to conquer. He had gone to his minister for advice. "A pure mind in a pure body," minister Howell said, echoing the advice Joshua had received from his father. "Be steadfast, pray, and repeat your alphabet twenty-five times before sunrise and twenty-five times before sleep." Joshua did as he was told but increased the number to fifty. He practiced reading aloud and, when he could corral them, read to his two younger brothers, Thomas and John.

"Well done," said Joshua's father, breaking into the boy's thoughts. "Let us rest. When the time is right, we'll put you to work in timber or the brickyards in Portland. That will build a mighty muscle or two."

Joshua set his sword against the spreading oak tree that grew in back of the Chamberlain farmhouse. Its russet and green leaves gave afternoon shade to the kitchen. "M-m-m-mother d-d-dreams I'll be a m-m-m-minister."

"Even ministers need strength. Your mother will come to realize that in time."

As if on cue, the rich voice of Sara Chamberlain rang from the back door. "Come in. Come in," she called. "Supper is ready!"

John and Tom, both with ravenous appetites, tumbled through the door, flinging themselves into the bare wooden chairs set around the simple table. Their father, too, feeling a rumble in his belly, followed with long, quick strides. Joshua was not far behind.

Chapter 2

Joshua Comes of Age

"I don't know if I can p-p-ass my tests but I'll d-d-d-do my v-v-very b-b-b-b-best," stammered Joshua, the schoolboy. He was preparing for final exams.

As Joshua grew taller and stronger he continued his efforts to overcome the dreadful stutter that had marked his life. He worked hard, practicing oratory and writing, and continued to repeat his alphabet upon rising and at nightfall. Eventually his self-discipline won him the prize he sought, and by the age of eighteen he was able to take a job as a teacher in the rural hamlet of North Milford, not far from the family farm.

While he taught and tutored Latin, Greek, mathematics and rhetoric, he studied hard to fulfill the lifetime dream of gaining entrance to Bowdoin College in Maine.

*   *   *

It was a time of wood-splitting and head-splitting. Joshua, always mindful of the words of the Greek philosopher, Plato . . . *a sound mind in a sound body* . . . worked harder than ever.

"Why do you want to become a Bowdoin man?" asked Professor Leonard Wood, head of the admissions committee.

"Because one of my great heroes is a Bowdoin graduate."

"And who might that be?"

"The inspiring writer, Nathaniel Hawthorne."

"Ah, yes," said Professor Wood. "That most admired American writer – he of *The Scarlett Letter, The House of Seven Gables, Twice-Told Tales* . . . "

Joshua interrupted. "Yes, sir, and *The Fall of the House of Usher*!"

"Have you actually read any of these books?"

"All sir. Every one."

Professor Wood seemed impressed. "Well, young man, we will push you to your limit. I hope you have an endless capacity for work and a deep thirst for knowledge, for with the effort will come the privilege of being known as a Bowdoin man."

*   *   *

Joshua gained a reputation as a hard working and passionate student during his years at Bowdoin. He was a true scholar, excelling in every subject. Although his reputation was richly deserved, his Puritan temperament, coupled with a preference for solitude, soon led his classmates to exclude him from their social functions. Fortunately, others admired his solid Yankee character and he became known to his teachers, and some of his classmates, as a man who could accomplish anything he set out to do.

During the springtime of his sophomore year, the school was engulfed in an ugly scandal. Some of the elite students had joined with others in a boisterous and rowdy night on the town. Joshua was summoned to the office of Leonard Wood, now President of the college.

"Mr. Chamberlain," the voice was stern and heavy with authority, "which students were involved in the lewd and drunken brawl that took place last night?"

Joshua was expressionless. He stared at a spot on the wall just above the President's head and kept his silence.

"If you remain silent, Mr. Chamberlain, I will be forced to suspend you. Immediately!"

"I refuse to answer the question," Joshua replied in a level voice. "I will not betray my classmates by being an informant. A traitor."

"Then," the President cleared his throat, "you are hereby suspended for an indefinite time. Pack your belongings and vacate the premises." President Wood's voice resounded throughout the bleak and silent room.

"Yes, sir!" Without a word of complaint or protest, Joshua Chamberlain executed a perfect about-face and marched out of the President's office. By the time he left the campus, word of his loyalty and steadfastness spread throughout the student dormitories. Within days, the guilty boys responsible for the scandal, and impressed by Joshua's loyalty and friendship, confessed to their errant behavior.

Realizing that Chamberlain's honor and demeanor had inspired his classmates to own up to their misdeeds, President Wood reinstated him.

But his return to the college was temporary. Shortly after this incident, Joshua was gripped by a mysterious illness. The ravages of this unknown disease wracked his body and spirit, and he lay near death growing weaker day by day.

For months, the doctors ordered complete bed-rest. This was followed by a rigorous schedule of exercise and special nutrients, leading, at last, to a full recovery. Joshua had missed a full year of schoolwork. He set his keen mind to the task of catching up and more than achieved his goal by relentless study. In his senior year, he was elected to Phi Beta Kappa, the oldest and most prestigious academic society in the country.

His mother still had hopes of Joshua becoming a minister. Honoring his mother's wishes, he enrolled in the Bangor Theological Seminary where he studied for three additional years, training for the ministry. Joshua assumed the duties of a minister, but after a brief attempt at teaching at the church's Sunday School, he realized that the religious life was not his calling. He knew exactly what he wanted to do. He wanted to be a teacher – and at what better place to fulfill his dream than his alma mater – Bowdoin College.

Chapter 3

Fireside Stories

Joshua Lawrence Chamberlain stepped into the office of College President, Leonard Wood, the same straight-laced man who had suspended him a few short years ago.

"Ah, Mr. Chamberlain. Are you ready for your oration?"

"Yes, sir."

"I seem to recall that at your graduation you were chosen to give the commencement speech. They say you stammered and seemed tongue-tied."

Joshua tightened his mouth but kept his composure. It was an unpleasant reminder of his stuttering days. "That is no longer a problem, sir. I am confident that I will do well."

Wood looked down at Joshua's application form resting on his mahogany desk. "I see that you have mastered several languages."

"Yes, sir. I am prepared to teach logic, theology, rhetoric and oratory, as well as nine languages, both ancient and modern."

"Very impressive. And what is your goal – your mission on behalf of your students?"

Joshua had spent many hours thinking of the answer to this question. President Wood was asking him why he wanted to teach. "I want to help my students, the gifted as well as the faltering. I want to challenge them, capture their imaginations . . . instill in them a love for learning . . . help them reason . . . think as well as act. I want them to achieve excellence and mastery in their chosen fields. I want to strengthen their backs . . . and their brains." Joshua thought he detected a faint smile on professor Wood's stony face, a barely noticeable sign of approval.

"Well, Mister Chamberlain, I think you have come to the right place. I'm sure that we can educate and advise you on the path to your lofty goals . . . *if,* and that is a big *if* . . . you pass your required oratory speech. Did you give any thought to its title and theme?"

"Yes, sir," replied Joshua. "Law and Liberty. Law without liberty is tyranny, and liberty without law is chaos."

"Impressive and interesting. Have you already begun the writing?"

"Written and re-written, sir. As you very well know, good writing is in the re-writing."

"You may wish to add the sentiments of one of our Founding Fathers, Benjamin Franklin, who warned us that *Any society that sacrifices liberty for safety and security deserves neither safety nor security . . . nor liberty.*"

"Thank you, professor. I shall add that to the main body of my oratory."

"Then there is no obstacle to keep you from joining our esteemed faculty. It seems that you advocate a liberal education as one of our beloved teachers did before you. Someone who taught modern languages, just as you will."

"And who might that be, sir?"

"Oh, young man, I was sure that you had read Henry Wadsworth Longfellow."

*   *   *

Success came easily to Joshua. Immersed in the academic life at Bowdoin, he became one of its most respected members, admired by both students and faculty.

But all the study and academic growth could not protect Joshua from the growing schism that was threatening the United States.

*   *   *

Calvin Stowe, a friend and fellow faculty member, as well as a Bowdoin graduate, often invited Joshua and other professors and intellectuals to his home in Brunswick. It became the site of many heated discussions involving that hot-button issue: Slavery and the Federal Union.

Calvin Stowe took an active part in these discussions, but it was his wife who was gaining even greater recognition for her fiery views on the evils of American slavery. Her name was Harriet Beecher Stowe.

One evening, when Joshua and Calvin were walking toward the Stowe house, Joshua said, "I understand, sir, that Mrs. Stowe has been teaching the local children and reading Sir Walter Scott to them – and to your own youngsters as well."

"Yes," replied the good Mr. Stowe. "The children are quite taken with *Ivanhoe*, Scott's imaginative tale of medieval chivalry."

"Excellent. Children should be encouraged to use their imaginations." Joshua turned to Professor Stowe. "I know your wife's views on the wickedness of slavery. She is a forceful and persuasive speaker – and, I hear, an excellent writer."

"No more than her brother, Henry Ward Beecher. He is a minister at a Congregational parish. It would do well for more of our citizens to hear the fire and brimstone sermons he favors, condemning all who endorse slavery to the hottest corner of hell."

"Where is his congregation?"

"Brooklyn, New York."

"Indeed. Word has it that when he speaks at rallies against slavery, thousands of citizens come out to support the cause."

The two men quickened their pace. They could see the oil lamp glowing in the window of the Stowe residence. It was like a beacon drawing them to hearth and hospitality, and to the pleasures of good and lively discussion.

The early winter snowfall had ended, and the crunch of their booted feet on the luminous snow could be heard for a distance on the clear and icy Maine night.

*   *   *

When Joshua and Calvin entered the parlor, the guests had already gathered around the wood-burning fireplace. Harriet Beecher Stowe, the only woman, held her hands out to the fire for warmth. A diminutive woman, hair coiled in a bun, she wore a simple cotton dress dyed a deep saxony blue, softened by a bit of lace around her throat. The four petticoats under her dress made her seem more substantial than she was.

Her husband looked at her kindly. A cautious man, he warned her, "Harriet, my dear, you're sitting much too close to the fire. Take care. With all those petticoats, you will attract the flames."

Harriet, an independent and assertive woman, shrugged. She made her own decisions. If she chose to sit near the fire, she would. But she softened at her husband's concern and drew back her chair . . . a mite.

"Well, gentlemen," she said, plunging into the evening's agenda, "shall we begin our discussion? Who has something to share that is newsworthy?"

Joshua spoke. "Jefferson Davis, our distinguished senator from Mississippi, will be the featured speaker at our commencement exercises this year. He will receive an honorary law degree." Joshua's face was serious. "I believe he has suggested that Maine secede from the Union and unite with Canada."

Harriet Beecher Stowe looked alarmed. "He couldn't have been serious."

"He's not the sort to jest."

"We are all well aware of the scurrilous intentions of the South if the question of slavery cannot be resolved," said Calvin Stowe.

"I am convinced that if there must be a war we are honor bound to take arms against the South and slavery." Joshua was grim.

"Our college president, Dr. Wood, has said that scholars have more important things to do than fight wars," interjected a professor of ancient history.

"Besides, you're too old to fight, Joshua. You're almost thirty," added the mathematics professor.

"I am determined," Joshua replied. "Remember the words of our fellow New Englander, Senator Daniel Webster: *Liberty and union, now and forever, one and inseparable.*"

The room became hushed.

Harriet Beecher Stowe broke the shroud of silence. "Well, gentlemen, shall we move on? I have planned my own activity for tonight."

"And what might that be, my dear?" asked her husband.

"Tonight I am going to read from my latest work, a serialized story that will soon appear in the *Atlantic Monthly.*"

"May I ask its title, my dear?"

"I haven't completely decided, but I am thinking of calling it *Uncle Tom's Cabin.*"

Chapter 4

The Winter of Secession: The Civil War

The rumble of secession had grown louder by the late 1850's. It seemed that nothing could stop the headlong plunge into war.

In October, 1859, the fanatic abolitionist, John Brown, captured the federal arsenal at Harper's Ferry, Virginia. Brown and his loyal band of eighteen were apprehended by Federal troops under the command of Colonel Robert E. Lee and Lieutenant J.E.B. Stuart. Brown was quickly tried and sentenced to death for treason.

Maine newspapers reported the events in rich detail, and Joshua read the papers avidly. He and Calvin Stowe were seated in comfortable leather chairs in the smoking lounge of the great hall at Bowdoin. Joshua shrugged. "The deed is done, I'm afraid."

The distant tolling of church bells cast a pall over the campus. Black bunting hung from all the buildings. "Will you be going to the memorial prayer meeting this afternoon?" asked Stowe.

"Yes. The man deserves it." Joshua glanced at the date at the top of the newspaper's banner – December 3, 1859, the day after John Brown was hanged. "Mister John Brown is now a martyr, left to the ages. The papers say that he called his hanging a 'public murder' and went to the gallows with great composure, almost cheerfulness."

Stowe shook his head sadly. "There are those who say that the hanging of John Brown will make the gallows as glorious as the cross."

"Only in the north, among hard bitten abolitionists like William Lloyd Garrison. The south will be an entirely different story."

Joshua was right. The death of John Brown split the nation in two. Throughout the south heightened fear of multiple slave rebellions led to a "reign of terror" as anti-slavery sentiments were violently suppressed, feeding the flames of the "irrepressible conflict."

There was no turning back.

The election of Abraham Lincoln in November of 1860 and his inauguration in March of the following year was the final straw for the rebels and led to the winter of secession. South Carolina seceded from the Federal Union, followed by Virginia, North Carolina, Georgia, Florida, Alabama, Mississippi, Louisiana, Texas, Tennessee and Kentucky. These eleven Confederate States of America elected Jefferson Davis as their president, the same senator who gave the graduation address and received an honorary law degree from Bowdoin College.

On April 12, 1861, the rebels fired on Fort Sumter, the Federal stronghold in South Carolina. The war had begun.

*　　*　　*

President Lincoln called for volunteers for the Union Army. Talk of war was everywhere: in the streets, at the tobacconist, in the Stowe's parlor and in college dormitories.

Seated in the faculty smoking lounge, the ancient history professor pulled his chair closer to the fire. "This war will be over before you know it. One or two decisive battles, and the rebels will surrender."

The mathematics professor agreed. "We have more money, more men, and more equipment!"

"The Lord is on our side!"

"What do you think, Joshua?" asked Stowe.

Joshua had been thinking of nothing else. He smoothed his long mustache that drooped an inch below his jaw, "As far as I'm concerned, Calvin, it's political heresy. Secession cannot stand. The very integrity of the United States has been attacked." He looked deeply into his friend's eyes. "But it is not going to be easy and it is not going to be brief. This war will be long and bloody. The rebels will be fighting on their own soil, on familiar territory. They are strong warriors, fighting for a cause in which they believe."

When Calvin Stowe replied, his voice was angry. "Backwoods warriors doing the devil's work under the cover of cotton and Spanish moss!"

"Much more than that," replied Joshua. "They'll be fighting for their homes, their sovereignty, their culture and civilization."

"I suppose you're right."

Joshua gazed into the fire. "Oh, the north will win. But our nation can only be united, or rather re-united, by bloodshed . . . by a terrible and bloody war that will cost more than many will be able to bear."

*   *   *

During those troubled times, Fletcher Webster, the son of Senator Daniel Webster, wrote new words to an old Protestant hymn. He called it *John Brown's Body*. It quickly became the marching song of the Union army or, as the soldiers sometimes referred to themselves, the Army of the Potomac.

The noted abolitionist, Julia Ward Howe, heard the song and wrote new lyrics for it. She titled the new song *The Battle Hymn of the Republic*. It was published in the *Atlantic Monthly* and quickly became President Lincoln's favorite.

Many students left school to join the army and save the Union. Joshua, too, was eager to volunteer.

His good friend, Calvin Stowe, reminded him, "You're thirty-three, Joshua, not a boy of eighteen anymore. All you've commanded is a classroom and a great deal of respect. That's hardly enough training for a difficult and treacherous war."

"Before I fight a war, I'll have to fight my friends, my family, and my colleagues," laughed Joshua, trying to allay his friend's worries. "I really don't know yet, Calvin. I haven't decided." But he did not deceive himself. He had, indeed, decided.

Cover of the 1862 sheet music for "The
Battle Hymn of the Republic"

Score

*One version of the melody, in C major, begins as below. This
is an example of the mediant-octave modal frame.*

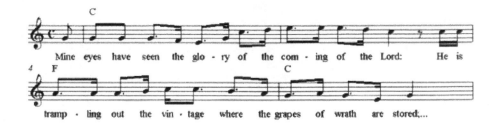

Lyrics

Mine eyes have seen the glory of the coming of the Lord:

He is trampling out the vintage where the grapes of wrath are stored;

He hath loosed the fateful lightning of His terrible swift sword:

His truth is marching on.

Chapter 5

Joshua Joins The Union Army

The early months of the Civil War were disastrous for the Union Army. The first major battle of the war was the Battle of Bull Run, at Manassas Junction. Hundreds of citizens, thinking the war was just another entertainment, a game to enjoy like a three-legged race, and expecting a quick and decisive Union victory, gathered at the heights of Bull Run. Many arrived by horse and buggy, bringing blankets and picnic baskets. They spread their quilts and blankets, unpacked their food and beverages, and prepared to enjoy the spectacle.

They were horrified to discover the brutal and murderous truth. Rifles and cannonades exploded, deafening the spectators. Dead and wounded soldiers, some no more than sixteen years of age, littered the unholy battlefield. Body parts of men and horses catapulted through the smoky air, landing on what once were grassy knolls. The wails and agony of the dying and wounded were a fitting lament to the nightmare that was the Civil War.

Stray minie balls and cannon shells struck some of the spectators. One of them burned to death – a woman wearing four ruffled petticoats under her gingham dress. An errant shell exploded nearby setting her petticoats on fire. The screams of the unlucky woman were drowned out by the repeated explosions. Frances Appleton, she was the wife of the celebrated American poet, Henry Wadsworth Longfellow.

When Joshua heard the tragic news, he was struck by the prophetic words of Calvin Stowe – "Harriet, my dear, you're sitting much too close to the fire. Take care. With all those petticoats, you'll attract the flames."

When the smoke had settled, the Confederate army was victorious and the Federal forces were in full retreat.

The decisive moment was at hand.

* * *

The next day, against all advice from friends, family and colleagues, Joshua stepped into President Leonard Wood's ornate office and requested a two year leave of absence from his teaching responsibilities at Bowdoin.

Dr. Wood was taken by surprise. He felt that Joshua was too much of an asset, too valuable, for the college faculty to lose. "For what purpose, Professor Chamberlain?"

"I plan to travel and study in Europe," fibbed Joshua.

Wood's face lit with delight and relief. "Splendid! This should push those foolish ideas about joining the army out of your head. Scholars teach. They do not fight."

"Then you are granting my request?"

"Absolutely, my good man. Absolutely. Travel and study in Europe can only enrich a mind such as yours, broaden your perspective and hone your skills as a teacher."

"Thank you, sir."

In less than a month, Joshua Lawrence Chamberlain, desperate to save his precious Union, volunteered for the Army of the Potomac. It was March of 1862. He was thirty-four years old.

With no military training or experience, he was appointed Assistant Commander of the 20th Maine Regiment, a Lieutenant Colonel, leading more than nine hundred proud and tough Maine Yankees. If ever an untried soldier got a crash course in military tactics and strategy, it was Lt. Colonel Joshua Lawrence Chamberlain.

RE-ENFORCE
M'CLELLAN!

RALLY FOR THE UNION!

STAND BY THE FLAG!

LET THE SONS OF MAINE FILL UP THEIR REGIMENTS!!

VOLUNTEERS WANTED!

One month's pay in advance; $55 to be paid each soldier before leaving the State, $100 and 160 acres of Bounty Land at the close of the war. Thirteen Non-Commissioned Officers to be appointed from the company.

Recruiting Office at John Staples' House, Bancroft Mills.

JOHN STAPLES,

Recruiting Officer.

Chapter 6

Kill The Brave Ones

Joshua learned quickly. He applied his great intelligence to mastering the art of military science and tactics, swiftly developing a command presence – determined, always, to lead his troops, and never shout orders from behind the ranks. He would not demand anything of them that he would not himself do.

By September of 1862, Lt. Colonel Chamberlain, second in command of the 20th Maine Regiment, was stationed at another burial ground for the Union Army – Antietam.

Under the command of Colonel Ames, the 20th Maine was kept in reserve soon to be plunged into a baptism of fire at Boteler's Ford. Joshua proved himself cool under fire and immediately gained the respect and admiration of his men.

The battle at Antietam made veterans overnight of the untested 20th Maine. They drilled for many hours, day and night, rain or shine. It was a challenge for Joshua who spent the best part of his day seated on a rock-hard saddle.

By early December Joshua's troops were on the move again, marching into the snow-blanketed northern Virginia countryside. Colonel Ames astride his chestnut stallion warned, "Prepare to see some heavy action during this campaign."

"Joshua reined in his favorite horse, Charlemagne. "Yes, sir," he replied, "that's what we came for."

The horses' hoofs were muffled by the pristine snow as the troops moved forward. "Don't you find the names of some Southern towns and villages quite amusing? Can you imagine, *Snicker's Gap* or *Vinegar Bend* in Maine?" Joshua smiled.

Colonel Ames chuckled. "Yes, I suppose they do sound funny to Yankee ears. Here's something that may interest and amuse you."

"I can use a good laugh."

"It's about your old friend Harriet Beecher Stowe."

Joshua was surprised. "Harriet?"

"The one and only, Miss Independent. Seems she met President Lincoln recently at the White House. Can you guess what the gentleman said to her?"

"I have no idea."

"Lincoln said, *'So this is the little lady who started this big war!'*".

"Do you really think *Uncle Tom's Cabin* had that great an impact on the country?"

"Who's to say? But her latest literary work may leave her previous book in the dust."

"So I've heard," said Joshua. "The new novel, *Pearl of Orr's Island*, is a passionate plea for the emancipation of women. While we men are fighting this accursed war, the women are becoming more independent, freed from the shackles of men's expectations."

"Well spoken. Here we are, fighting to emancipate the slaves, while the women struggle to emancipate themselves. But one thing at a time," said Ames, "the women will have to wait."

"I wonder," countered Joshua, "some of them have fine principles and strong minds. Who knows? They may change the world if given a chance."

The two officers settled into a comfortable silence. Only Charlemagne broke the peace with an occasional snort.

Ames spoke. "I believe we're going to have some new concerns in the next few days. The rebel army, led by General Stonewall Jackson, will be waiting for us. Did you hear what he said when his men asked who to fire upon first?"

"No, tell me."

"General Jackson, that excellent, God-fearing man said, *'Kill the brave ones, they lead the others.'*"

Joshua felt a chill run down his spine not caused by the frigid night. "Sound military advice. I guess that keeps me safe."

"I suspect you have more to worry about than most."

"That remains to be seen. Where do you think we'll find the General?"

Colonel Ames tugged at his field cap. "Probably at Fredericksburg – at the stone wall that runs through it."

*　　*　　*

Fredericksburg. The 20th Maine, under the command of Colonel Ames and Lt. Colonel Chamberlain, approached the river which cut through the valley leading to the rebel stronghold.

Joshua reined in his horse at the river's edge. "Where are the pontoons? Who's in command here!"

"McClellan has been replaced by Burnside," replied Ames. "President Lincoln believes McClellan is too cautious. He wants a more aggressive commander to lead the Union Army. Camp gossip has it that McClellan has more heart than head."

"That could be a danger, sir. General McClellan is well loved by his men. If he asked them to march on Washington, they would. They could overthrow the president. The country would be torn apart, two countries – the United States and the Confederacy." Joshua drew a deep breath.

Ames thought about this possible turn of events. "No," he said, "McClellan would never do that. He loves his country too well. What's more, he hasn't the heart to be a military dictator. He'll be loyal. You mark my words." The two men were lost in thought, thinking how fragile their beloved nation had become.

The sound of axes chopping through wood could be heard. The crash of falling trees, familiar to every Maine man, echoed in the near distance. The troops fanned out at the river's edge, and turned their thoughts to home.

Army engineers were building pontoons for the river crossing. Joshua was angry. "There's been far too much delay. Those pontoons should have been built days ago!"

As each day passed, and the pontoons were not completed, the Maine regiment and the entire 5th Corps, under the new command of Daniel Butterfield, grew more and more restless.

Finally at dawn, on December 13, 1862, Burnside, the new commander, ordered the troops to cross the river and confront the enemy.

Joshua heard the reports of relentless rifle fire and the deafening explosions of a massive artillery barrage.

"Get the men ready," ordered Ames. "The rebels hold the high ground. We are fully exposed."

"What do we do?" asked a frightened young private. Joshua recognized Ronald O'Keefe, the only son of one of his closest friend's, Dr. Martin O'Keefe.

Joshua forced a smile to reassure the boy. "We attack, private. We attack."

Once across the river, without hesitation, Chamberlain led his regiment, plunging them into a nightmare of unrelenting firepower – raging sheets of flame, a hell-storm . . . a bloodbath.

The battlefield was littered with the unlucky. The gray shirts had triumphed again. The Union blue lay slaughtered like cattle. The troops that survived retreated, running from the devastation.

Daniel Butterfield, 5th Corps commander, ordered the men to regroup and attack again. Joshua faithfully executed the order. Brandishing his saber, he led his decimated troops in a desperate and futile charge. The foray collapsed and the Union soldiers yielded the field to the rebels superior position.

Night fell and a bone-chilling cold settled in. The exhausted troops used the bodies of their fallen comrades to warm and protect them. Nobody slept.

*   *   *

Joshua ordered his men to pile the dead around them to form a temporary fortress. Lt. Colonel Chamberlain belly-crawled among his men that night: He pressed his canteen to the lips of the wounded. "Soldier, drink some water. Here, let me loosen those bandages." He tried to console and encourage the heroic men. "Can I write to somebody for you, soldier?" He recorded the last words of the dying, bringing hope and some measure of comfort to the young and the lost.

I am in a bone-garden, he thought as he lay there, huddled among the mangled and the dead, praying for some heavenly spark to fight the brain-numbing chill.

At dawn, the assault began anew – the dull thud of bullets violating the breastwork of corpses. The shrieks and moans of the newly wounded pierced the fragile air. The funeral march of exhausted men continued.

An order came from Butterfield's 5th Corps command, "Retreat!"

The battered remnants of the 20th Maine lifted themselves from the now blood-stained snow, staggering from their humiliating defeat.

The Confederates having wreaked havoc upon the Union Army vacated Fredericksburg, and the 5th Corp, like ghost walkers, entered a deserted city.

That night the 20th Maine slept on the cold streets of Fredericksburg. The next day Joshua led his men again, this time in an orderly retreat out of Fredericksburg. The Union Army surgeons, those angels of mercy, stayed behind to treat the wounded.

*   *   *

Fighting Joe Hooker, senior corps commander, spurred his horse and galloped up to Joshua. "You've had a hard time of it, Colonel. I'm glad to find you alive."

Dog tired and in no mood to exchange polite conversation, Joshua snapped, "It was chance, General, not much intelligent design."

"Are you blaming me?" Hooker's voice was sharp. "God knows that I did not give the order to send you in."

"That was the trouble, General. You should have given the order. You should have put more of us into the battle, the whole Army of The Potomac, if necessary. Instead we were thrown like appetizers into the devil's gaping jaws."

General Hooker, unaccustomed to such outrageous arrogance from a junior officer, stiffened, wheeled his horse around and galloped off.

Joshua spotted the young private, Ronald O'Keefe. "I'm pleased to see you are still with us, soldier."

"Thank you, sir," replied the young man. "I, too, am pleased – perhaps a bit more pleased than you, sir."

Joshua smiled. This time the smile was genuine. Feeling good for the first time in months, Joshua walked back to his canvas tent.

The 20th Maine stayed bivouacked for most of the winter. They were not called upon again until early May, 1863. Joshua put them through their usual drills to keep them battle ready and uplift their spirits.

He was saddened and troubled to see how thin the ranks had become after Fredericksburg, but consoled by the sight of those who had borne the brunt of the battle and survived. The smiling and trusting face of private Ronald O'Keefe, only son of his dearest friend, particularly cheered him.

*　　*　　*

Joshua's youngest brother, Tom, joined the 20th regiment as a junior officer. Soon after, in January 1863, there was an outbreak of smallpox. The men were quarantined. but most were eager to rejoin the fight. Tom was particularly impatient. "If we can't do anything else," he sulked, "at least we could give them the smallpox!"

Joshua smiled. But instead of rejoining the battle, his regiment was ordered to guard the telegraph lines and Federal emplacements, thus missing a crushing defeat at Chancellorsville.

As the 20th Maine departed the outskirts of Chancellorsville, two exciting bits of gossip circulated among the men. Thomas 'Stonewall' Jackson was mortally wounded. One of his own men, a confedcrate sentry mistaking Jackson for a Union soldier, nervously shot the general. It was known that General Robert E. Lee had lamented: *I have lost my strong right arm.*

Joshua commented, "Well, Ol' Stonewall encouraged his men to kill the bravest. I guess they were just obeying orders."

The second was that Colonel Ames was promoted to Brigade Commander and his replacement as Regimental Commander was the level-headed and courageous Joshua Lawrence Chamberlain.

Chapter 7

Brother Against Brother

The Civil War pitted neighbor against neighbor, friend against friend, brother against brother. Scouting reports confirmed that a Rebel commander, General Heth, in search of shoes for his ragged division, led it into a small town in southeastern Pennsylvania. As Heth's troops filtered into town, they clashed with a detachment of Union cavalry. Battle flared. Although the conflict was unplanned, it burgeoned into a raging massacre as forces from both sides poured into the sleepy town of Gettysburg.

A month after the slaughter at Chancellorsville, Regimental Commander Joshua Lawrence Chamberlain and his troops were on the move again. This time, in the direction of Pennsylvania. As they neared Gettysburg, Joshua spotted a Union Calvary officer speeding toward him at full gallop. "Whoa," he ordered Charlemagne, bringing the regiment to a halt.

"Sir," shouted the officer, "I have orders from General Meade!"

"Read them."

"There are some mutineers in the 2nd Maine Regiment and I have been ordered to leave them in your charge. General Meade has ordered that you make them perform their duties or, if they refuse, shoot them down."

"Thank you. I'll take over from here." The Calvary officer saluted. Joshua, with a snap of his wrist, returned the salute as the young officer wheeled his horse around and sped off in the direction of Gettysburg.

George Meade was yet another commander of the Army of the Potomac chosen by President Lincoln in his frantic search for a general who could bring honor to the north and change the course of the war.

Joshua considered the fate of the mutineers. Then he summoned his brother, Tom. "I am placing you in charge of the deserters, Lieutenant. I don't want to lose another moment in our march to Gettysburg."

"Yes, sir!" Lieutenant Thomas Chamberlain respected and admired his older brother and always treated him with full military courtesy. Later that night, Tom assembled the mutineers. He walked among them, paused to ask their names and hometowns, and directed that food and beverage be brought.

Having done that, he spoke in a calm, self-assured voice. "Men, I have orders to shoot you down if you refuse to submit and rejoin the ranks. I have given much thought to the matter and have decided that it is better not to carry out these orders. I know that you have faced some very difficult and painful times in this awful war and you have your reasons for refusing to fight, but so have my men. Our ranks are woefully thin. We lost a lot of boys in Fredericksburg, but the rest have stayed the course and paid the price. We can use your help. I am *asking* for your help. The regiment marches at dawn. I hope you will march with us."

That night the men of the 20th Maine drifted off to sleep in an open field, under a star-studded sky. They were listening, for the first time, to a melody that brought peace to their hearts and tears to their eyes. The music, composed by General Daniel Butterfield, eased from the bugle and blanketed the tired men.

The 20th Maine honored their division commander by naming it *Butterfield's Lullaby*. In time it became immortal, and was known to every man who ever served as *Taps*.

In the morning, the Union men, including the deserters from the 2nd regiment, assembled on the grassy field to join Regimental Commander Joshua Chamberlain on the long march to Gettysburg.

Joshua heard the rumble of distant thunder – the distinct and unmistakable sound of an artillery barrage countered by artillery cannonade, and he thought – *Gettysburg*.

At that moment, a horseman, whipping his steed as though he carried an urgent message, came to a dust-raising halt in front of Joshua. "Welcome to Gettysburg, sir."

"How goes the battle?"

"We have already lost our 1st Corp Commander, sir. General Reynolds was killed yesterday, cut down by a rebel sharpshooter."

"Who is in command?"

"General Abner Doubleday."

"Doubleday? Isn't he the man who claims to have invented that new game? What does he call it?"

"Baseball, I think, sir."

Joshua nodded. "Baseball, you say. We will see what comes of it. Likely, it will be a passing fad like so many others – but General Doubleday is a bright and capable leader. I have a good deal of respect for him."

"Colonel, before we speak further, I am to tell you to get your men to the battlefield at once. Doubleday, the Union Army and Gettysburg need you desperately!"

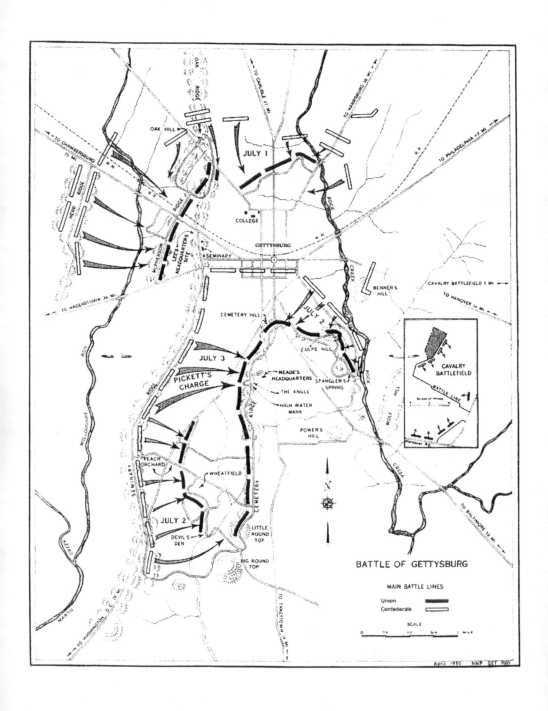

BATTLE OF GETTYSBURG

MAIN BATTLE LINES

Union
Confederate

SCALE
0   1/4   1/2   3/4   1 MILE

Chapter 8

The Battle for the Little Round Top

On July 2, 1863, the 20th Maine joined with other units of the Army of the Potomac. Colonel Strong Vincent, Joshua's brigade commander, spurred his horse and rushed to meet them. "I sure am glad to welcome you boys. We need every able-bodied man we can muster."

Joshua saluted his superior officer. "Thank you, sir. The 20th Maine is ready and eager to fight. How is the battle going?"

"It's shaping up to be the big one. Biggest of the war. The rebels will be fighting like devils now, especially after hearing of President Lincoln's plan. Obviously you've already heard about it?"

"Yes, sir. Everyone has."

Colonel Strong Vincent ran his thumb across his mouth. "Lincoln's Emancipation Proclamation frees only the slaves in those states still in rebellion against the United States."

"What of the slaves in the loyal border states like Maryland and Missouri?"

"No action there. Our president does not want to provoke those states. Ol' Abe has no immediate plans to free them."

Joshua, the military strategist, assessed the situation. Lincoln was doing nothing to antagonize those states who had sworn allegiance to the Federal Union. He planned to free only the slaves in the Confederacy. Since the Confederacy recognized Jefferson Davis, not Lincoln, as their president, they would simply ignore the proclamation – but they would be outraged by Lincoln's manipulative affront and fight even harder for their cause.

Joshua's reaction was strong. "Sir," he said to the colonel, "I volunteered to suppress a rebellion and preserve our Federal Union. Now I am fighting a crusade to end the scourge of slavery. Surely you know that can only be accomplished with a complete Union victory."

"Well said, Colonel Chamberlain. Let us begin the crusade!"

Joshua scanned the Union positions. The vast expanse of the Gettysburg battlefield was revealed Still visible were the remains of the first day's carnage. He saw where the lines had broken and, in some cases, disintegrated. Yet, he felt the stir of battle just beginning.

Colonel Strong Vincent swept the field with his binoculars. "Damn!"

"Sir?" asked Joshua picking up Vincent's concern.

Vincent peered at two hills. "Robert E. Lee is probably discovering those hills even as we speak."

"Sir?" repeated Joshua, aware of Vincent's growing alarm.

"Our far left flank is unprotected. Our entire army is in peril. The men are clear targets. They are virtually hanging in air."

"Which two hills are you looking at, sir?"

Strong handed his field glasses to Joshua. "Take a look. There." He pointed to Little Round Top and Big Round Top. "Those two hills control the entire southern end of the battlefield. Why are they still unoccupied? If we controlled Little Round Top, we could observe the entire rebel army."

Joshua peered through the binoculars. "Yes, sir! Lee and his army would lose the element of surprise if we held the high-ground. He'd do anything to control Little Round Top!"

The two commanders exchanged knowing glances.

"Follow me," ordered Strong Vincent. His horse was running at a fast gallop before the words were out of his mouth.

Joshua turned to his men. "Let's go boys!"

The remnants of the 20th Maine raced at the heels of their Colonel. Little Round Top was strewn with boulders, jagged with sharp edges. The crest was bald with a few gnarled trees straggling down the sides.

The armies met, Confederate against Union.

The 20th deployed its weapons. Confederate artillery batteries opened fire. Splinters of rock, limbs of men and trees, shards of flying iron saturated the blackened air. The concussion of one cannonade almost tore Joshua out of his boots.

He turned to Tom who was at his side, "Brother, I don't like this. With both of us in the thick of battle, another shot like that might make it terribly hard on our mother"

"Our mother will be fine. Our father will be fine." Tom slapped Joshua's back. "The two of us will be fine."

Vincent beckoned Joshua to his side. "Your 20th Maine is our last line of defense. If the rebels conquer this position, the Federal line will be impossible to hold. We must win at any cost."

"I understand, sir."

"Remember, *at any cost*. No surrender. No retreat."

"You can rely on my Maine boys, sir."

"I know I can, Colonel Chamberlain. I know I can." Although he knew full well that General Meade would never have deployed a volunteer regiment commanded by a citizen soldier, a college professor at that, to defend the key position at Gettysburg. He had no choice and he knew it. "I must rejoin my Brigade. Good luck." Strong Vincent galloped off to his command amid a deafening bombardment of Rebel artillery fire.

Joshua called his officers into a huddle. "Boys, our regiment has been chosen to take the brunt of the rebel onslaught. The rebel mission is simple – to outflank us. If they do, the battle is doomed. Our mission is also simple – to stand up to them, man for man, bullet for bullet, bayonet for bayonet. Prevent them, at all cost, from deploying all outflanking maneuvers. Let them see what Maine men can do."

There was some buzzing among the officers.

"Deploy troops," shouted Joshua. "We occupy good ground. The rebels will have an uphill struggle."

"We'll be drastically outnumbered," said Tom.

"I expect about three to one. What about those mutineers from the 2nd Maine?"

"All have decided to fight."

"Good. We can use every man."

The 20th Maine, no more than three hundred men, fanned out across the crest of Little Round Top, taking positions behind every boulder, every gnarled tree, every rut.

Suddenly, the rebel artillery barrage ceased. A frontal attack was imminent.

"Anchor on the left flank." Joshua waited . . . and waited . . . and waited. "Here they come, boys!" he shouted. In the distance, across the open field, the thin gray line walked briskly.

Every Blue Coat crouched lower behind his concealment. "What rebel outfit are we facing, sir?" asked a young corporal.

Joshua stared into the distance and recognized the colors advancing toward them. "I believe we're about to meet General Longstreet's corps, spearheaded by Oates' crack 15th Alabama."

The rebel lines broke into a trot. A run. A sprint. The whoops and shouts grew louder as the direct frontal assault closed the gap.

"Patience, men," shouted Joshua. "Wait until you have a clear bead on the rebs. Don't waste ammunition."

Then, like a volcano, the battle erupted with wave after wave of molten lava sweeping over Little Round Top. The rebel infantry flowed uphill, beginning a death struggle that was to determine the fate of the Union.

Joshua concentrated the main bulk of his regiment where the attack was thickest. He grasped the warrior's sense of terrain, weapons and manpower. Standing tall at the summit, he shouted orders and words of encouragement to his troops.

The vanguard of the Confederate attack came clearly into view without benefit of cover. Joshua unsheathed his saber, raised it high and snapped it down. "Fire!" he ordered. "Fire for effect!"

A volley of searing musket balls ripped through the first wave of Confederates. Amidst the roar of musket, rifle and pistol fire, both Rebel and Federal troops fell, faces in dirt, beneath an indifferent sky.

The Rebels stormed the hill again and again but were turned back by the courage and granite determination of the 20th Maine. An eerie silence fell over the battlefield.

Joshua called to his brother. "Tom!"

"Yes, sir!

"Report!"

Tom faltered. "Weed . . . O'Rorke . . . Hazlett . . ."

Joshua braced himself for more bad news. "Out with it!"

"Strong Vincent is dead – cut down by a rebel sharpshooter."

"Bad news. Excellent man." Joshua cleared his throat. "Go on."

"We're low on ammo."

"How low?"

"Dangerously."

"Order the men to take ammo, cartridge belts and rifles from the dead. We will repulse any new attack with ammunition taken from the field."

"Do you think it will be soon?"

"You can wager a month's pay on it."

The words were barely out of Joshua's mouth, when primitive whoops and shouts were heard signaling a fresh attack. The Confederate regiment stormed the hill, grossly outnumbering the battered Federal troops.

Joshua strode up and down the lines rallying his faltering men. "Refuse the line! Refuse the line!" he shouted. The Maine boys fought valiantly, turning back the frantic Confederate attempts to outflank and overrun them.

Time and again the exhausted Yankees repulsed the rebel attacks. More slaughter. More carnage. More death. Soldiers lost their footing on the blood-soaked grass. Joshua moved among his dwindling troops steeling their resolve. "Hold fast men! Hold fast!"

A minie ball lodged in Joshua's leg. Another grazed his foot. *Pesky mosquitoes,* he thought.

In what seemed like hours, the second Rebel attack subsided and the 15th Alabama was ordered by Colonel Oates to reform and regroup. When the smoke cleared, the belly of the 20th Maine was gouged and bleeding.

Tom reported. "Joshua, we have only a scattering of men left and we are completely out of ammunition. Our situation is hopeless."

"Sir, can't we retire? Perhaps we can withdraw and be relieved," said Private O'Keefe, still among the lucky living.

Joshua surveyed the damage. Blue and Gray dead formed grotesque patterns along the crest of the hill. "Men!" he called. The desolate remnants of the once proud regiment circled their leader. "We are the last defense of the last army of the Republic. The Union Army ends with the 20th Maine. There is nobody to relieve us. The battle for the left flank of Little Round Top rests on your brave and capable shoulders."

"Sir, there is not a single cartridge or minie ball left in our regiment," said a shaken Private O'Keefe. "What do we do if the rebels attack?"

"Not *if*, private. *When* they attack."

"What are your orders, Colonel?" asked Tom.

Joshua's leg and foot throbbed from his wounds. He turned away from his troops and, for several moments, was lost in thought. He thought of what a favorite professor had taught him: "If we remember our history, we will be prepared for our future." Joshua remembered George Washington's brilliant tactical command decision. *When the odds are hopeless and there seems no chance of victory – attack.*

In 1776, on a freezing, wind-driven Christmas eve, General Washington crossed the raging Delaware River and attacked the

Hessians in Trenton. Of the original twenty thousand Continental troops, only three thousand had survived, many not fit for combat. Mostly New Englanders, many from Maine, they were far outnumbered by Hessian mercenaries. It was only through Yankee steadfast determination and courage that Washington's men turned certain defeat into a smashing victory.

Joshua faced his troops. "On my command, we attack!" He spat the words through clenched jaws. There was a murmur of disbelief from the troops.

"But, sir, what will we use for ammunition?"

"Bayonets."

"Bayonets!" exclaimed the incredulous men.

"When they attack, we counter attack. It's now or never. On my command, we will execute a right wheel forward."

"Sir, who will lead the attack?"

"I will," said Joshua. "Any questions?"

The boys from Maine were rendered mute.

Within minutes, the 15th Alabama had regrouped. They charged up Little Round Top amidst shrieking battle cries. Rifle and pistol fire were deafening.

Joshua waited for the precise moment before unsheathing his sword. It made a lethal flash in the bright Gettysburg sun.

"Bayonets!" he yelled over the din of shellfire. The 20th Maine, exhausted almost beyond human limits, flung itself down the hill with fixed bayonets.

Joshua, with the fury of a man possessed, hurtled down the hill towards the Rebels. A Confederate officer aimed his pistol point blank at his head.

The weapon misfired. Joshua, taking advantage of this stroke of luck, touched his sword to the officer's throat and nicked it with a flick of his wrist. The Confederate officer, quickly rethinking the situation, surrendered his saber and pistol to Colonel Chamberlain.

All along the line, hand-to-hand combat exploded and clashed until the 15th Alabama was shaken to its core. Shocked and bewildered by the death-defying counter attack, the Rebels panicked, broke ranks and fled in full disorderly retreat. On that brutal day every man of the 15th Alabama Regiment either surrendered or perished. A savage and bloody victory that would change the tide of the war was won in Gettysburg by Colonel Joshua Lawrence Chamberlain and the valiant men of the 20th Maine.

Chapter 9

Gettysburg: The Turning Point

After the battle, utter exhaustion overcame Joshua and the survivors of Little Round Top. A bedraggled remnant, less than two hundred men from an original roster of nine hundred, dragged themselves back to the main Union line as other Federal troops poured in to defend and occupy the strategic hill.

A senior commander, Colonel James Rice, drew up on his dark brown steed and stopped Joshua. "Allow me to salute you, sir"

"It is I who should salute you, sir," said Joshua to his superior officer.

"Not at all. I was in clear sight of Little Round Top during the worst of the fighting. The battle for Gettysburg hung on your line of defense. I am certain that you will be recommended for the Medal of Honor for valor and conspicuous gallantry far above the call of duty."

"Thank you, sir." Joshua, uncomfortable with praise, remained silent.

"We are moving your outfit to the center of Big Round Top, the safest spot in the Union line. Good luck." Rice turned his horse and galloped off to the line of defense assigned to his brigade.

Though there were a few minor skirmishes that moonlit Pennsylvania night, there were no further casualties. The 20th Maine were roused at dawn. After a quick field breakfast of black coffee and hardtack, they marched to Big Round Top. Joshua positioned his men and reported to Corps Commander, General Winfield Scott Hancock. The command post was in a small clapboard farmhouse next to an apple orchard.

"Congratulations, Colonel. I've been hearing a lot about your brilliant strategy . . . and your superb 20th Maine as well. The battle for Gettysburg is not yet over, but a Union victory will give new strength to our cause," said Hancock.

"Yes, sir. It will also shake the Rebel's confidence."

"I like what you're saying and the way you say." General Hancock clapped Joshua's shoulder and shook his hand

"What are my orders, sir?" Joshua was suddenly eager to rejoin his troops.

"I am placing you and your 20th Maine at Cemetery Ridge. You will be held in reserve behind the center of our main line of defense."

"Yes, sir." Joshua raised his right hand to the tip of his field cap and snapped a formal salute.

Hancock returned the ancient exchange of honor and respect. "Dismissed," he said, his voice crisp.

Joshua ordered his troops to Cemetery Ridge. The men fanned out along the main lines of Union defense, a safe distance behind

Hancock's Corps – but no soldier was guaranteed safety on that balmy day.

Within minutes, a thunderous Rebel artillery barrage shattered the fragile air. Weapons, ammunition, horses and soldiers were blown into the crumbling Gettysburg sky.

Union artillery batteries counter-engaged. Screams of the wounded, the shriek of flying missiles, the shrill song of destruction, came together like a thunderous wave, burying all in a sea of chaos.

Suddenly, the cannonade ceased. Silence engulfed them. Joshua trained his field glasses on the vast field beyond the breastworks and stone wall where Hancock's corps crouched and waited. A mile-wide army of what appeared to be black ants was swarming closer. Jonathan drew a deep breath. The worst was yet to come.

As the soldier ants grew larger, they were transformed into lethal weapons – General George Pickett's Confederate Division, part of General James Longstreet's invincible Corps.

Pickett's Division spearheaded the advance.

His long, gray line of soldiers moved slowly, then picked up considerable speed, then ran at full tilt, then . . . charged!

At precisely the right moment, under Hancock's order, the Federal defenders opened fire. A barrage of deadly minie balls, cannon and shrapnel projectiles decimated the first wave of Rebel attackers. The second wave met a similar fate. Some sections of the Rebel division faltered and stopped. Others retreated. Still others broke ranks and fled. But there were others who kept advancing despite the withering firestorm.

A brigade, led by General Lewis Armistead, breeched the stone wall and overran a section of the Union line.

What followed was brutal. Men and boys who once saluted the same flag, who once thought of themselves as friends and brothers, now, in hand-to-hand combat, were frenzied enemies, pitched in a violent struggle, wanting nothing more than to take each other's lives.

Hancock rallied his troops. The line was re-taken and secured. General Lewis Armistead was mortally wounded and Pickett's ill-fated charge was finally crushed. Of the 4,500 Rebels who charged the wall only eight hundred staggered back to Confederate lines, stunned and shocked.

Then, there arose a mighty roar. All along the Federal line infantry, artillery, cavalry and sharpshooters – many standing atop the stone wall, feet planted wide, rifles raised above their heads – shouted in choral unison: "Fredericksburg! Fredericksburg! Fredericksburg!"

Joshua stood with pride, his heart beating wildly, knowing that Chancellorsville, Fredericksburg and Bull Run had been avenged, and that the triumph at Gettysburg was a monumental turning point for the Union cause.

"Tom, get the boys ready. We've got Bobby Lee on the run. General Meade is sure to order a massive counter-attack."

Joshua and the 20th Maine waited in anxious anticipation for the order to destroy the army of Northern Virginia under General Robert E. Lee.

It never came.

Finally, late in the day, Joshua and the other Union Commanders were ordered to Hancock's headquarters. In less than an hour, Joshua returned. "General Meade has decided to rest the Army of the Potomac," he said. "He's allowing Lee to retreat unopposed."

"Unbelievable," said Tom. The dismay in his voice was clear.

"Lee can't retreat as fast as we can advance," Joshua replied to his brother. "Meade is playing it safe. Another opportunity to shorten this war has slipped through our fingers." Joshua thought: *Is Lincoln never going to choose a commander bold and brave enough to lead this great army?*

GETTYSBURG

Chapter 10

The Firing Squad

After the battle of Gettysburg Joshua fell victim to malaria. Delirium was his frequent companion. After a slow and painful recuperation, he returned to active duty.

Colonel James Rice, his friend and commander from Little Round Top, rode up to greet him. "How are you, Joshua?"

"Fit as a fiddle, James. Ready to re-join the fight."

"That's good news, Joshua, and I have further news. You have been promoted to 3rd Brigade Commander but without the customary promotion to general.

Joshua accepted the news with mixed emotions. He knew that he was often outspoken and that he had alienated some officials. He had been given a huge responsibility without the corresponding honor. And although personal ambition had little to do with it, the slap stung.

"Now I have some bad news," said Rice.

Joshua braced himself. "Let's have it, sir."

"You have been chosen to oversee and witness the execution of five Union boys."

Joshua's face darkened. "What was their crime?"

"Desertion in the face of duty."

"When does the execution take place?"

"Immediately," answered Rice. "No time like the present. Follow me."

Rice led Joshua beyond the parade field to a wooded patch of earth. Five young soldiers were digging holes in the ground. The horror of it struck Joshua. The doomed boys were digging their own graves.

"Enough!" rasped the sergeant in charge of the grizzly detail.

Then Joshua saw them – five pinewood caskets piled on a horse-drawn cart.

"Take 'em down and stand 'em up in front of the holes!" growled the sergeant pointing to the coffins. His voice was pitiless. Having witnessed so much brutality, so much death and destruction, he had shut off all human emotions.

"Those poor souls," Joshua whispered to Colonel Rice. "They must be so frightened."

"Everybody is scared, but few desert," replied Rice.

"Is there nothing we can do?"

"Too late for that."

Shuffling their feet, the hapless men removed the coffins from the cart, dragged them to their gravesites and stood them in front of the firing squad.

More than fifty men made up the execution detail. The condemned were ordered to stand in front of their coffins, The firing squad stood ready. Each man was blindfolded. The sergeant in charge looked at Joshua for his final order.

Joshua gazed at the young men who had proved incapable of carrying war's great burden. He paused, then, with a slight nod, gave the signal.

"Ready!" shouted the sergeant.

The firing squad, half kneeling, half standing, locked into position.

"Aim!"

More than fifty rifles pointed at human hearts.

"Fire!"

A volley of thunder shattered the air. Five men pitched into their caskets. Five caskets toppled into freshly dug earth.

Joshua shuddered. A thousand men dead were a statistic. Five, up close, were a tragedy.

Chapter II

Ulysses S. Grant: The Fighting Commander

Periodic bouts of malaria and pneumonia plagued Joshua for the rest of 1863 and into 1864, convincing many that his last hours were at hand. But he recovered and returned to duty. In battle, at Rappahannock Station, his horse was shot from under him, pitching him forward, flinging him to the ground. When he regained consciousness, he was drenched in the animal's blood.

One thundering battle blurred into another, but something significant happened, something that would change the course of the war. Lincoln appointed General Ulysses S. Grant as the overall commander of the Union Army.

Joshua rejoiced. "At last, we have a true commander – one who will fight, press on . . . and win!"

At the Wilderness Campaign, Joshua led his men into the woods and underbrush of Virginia, fighting some of the hardest, most brutal battles of the war. He spearheaded his brigade at the Spotsylvania Court House when Grant ordered the attack. During the bloodshed, he came across an old friend. He was a mortally wounded comrade, and a fellow warrior of Little Round Top.

Colonel James Rice lay dying, a jagged piece of shrapnel lodged in his chest. Blood rushed from the gaping wound. Joshua cradled the dying man. "James, my dear friend, is there anything I can do?"

"Turn my face to the enemy. Let me see, for the last time, how General Grant has hammered our foe."

Joshua gently turned his good friend to the south. Within seconds Colonel James Rice was dead.

Tears welled in Joshua's eyes. "The hammering has been harsh on the hammer," he whispered, saluting his fallen comrade.

The endless struggle continued. Bethesda Church. Pole Cat Creek. Somehow Joshua and others survived – his brother Tom, Private O'Keefe . . .

On the road to Richmond, the heart of the Confederacy, Joshua recklessly braved enemy fire. Tom, growing concerned for his brother's safety, said, "Sir, I know that you would ask nothing of us that you would not yourself do. Your disregard for your own welfare is legendary but if you can't consider your own safety, could you possibly consider the safety of . . . " he hesitated, at a loss for words . . . "Charlemagne?"

Joshua responded to the humor, "My dear younger brother and junior officer, Tom, it is necessary for a Brigade Commander to know everything that is going on despite his personal welfare."

"Well, Brigade Commander, sir, what killing field is next?"

"Looks like Cold Harbor."

Cold Harbor it was. Grant swung through Virginia and the Army of the Potomac followed. The heavy blow of the hammer struck relentlessly. The destruction of Rebel troops was severe but the sacrifice of Federal forces was stunning.

Joshua addressed his men before the final assault at Cold Harbor. "Boys, I want you to pin your names on your shirts." He did not have to explain the command. They would be easier to identify if they were killed in action. And killed they were. Twelve thousand perished in a day.

*   *   *

Petersburg. Joshua had hoped for a Union commander who was fearless and bold of heart. Be ever careful for what you wish; it may be granted. And it was – in the person of Ulysses Simpson Grant.

Petersburg was a meat grinder. One attack followed another. One order, in particular, was deadly: "Colonel Chamberlain," roared his immediate commanding officer, "you will attack the Rebel stronghold at Rives Salient."

"Sir! That order means suicide and certain defeat for my boys. It's a reckless waste of lives. I hope you will reconsider."

The Division Commander was stunned. His eyes flared. "Colonel, are you disobeying a direct order?"

"General, my men are isolated. The assault is futile."

The General struggled to regain his composure. He strode toward Joshua until they stood toe to toe. "I am reordering you to attack. Any disobedience will mean insubordination. Do I make myself clear?"

"Perfectly clear, General."

Gauging the danger, Joshua commandeered a chestnut mare from a fallen cavalry officer. He patted Charlemagne's rump. "Old friend," he said, "you're sitting this one out." He mounted the chestnut, unsheathed his saber and led his meager army into hell.

He had charged less than 60 yards when a cannonball exploded, killing the mare instantly and hurling Joshua to the ground. With seconds to recover, he bolted to his feet, retrieved his saber and sprinted toward the Rebel line. Private O'Keefe overtook him, shouting, "Sir! Sir! Stop! It's folly to lead on foot! You'll be exposed to mortal danger!"

"My sworn duty, O'Keefe. Now, let's get on with it!"

"I'm with you, sir."

A fifteen-year-old color bearer caught up to them. "Let's give them a good pounding, sir!"

Whump! The boy clutched his chest and fell dead at Joshua's feet, a minie ball through his reckless heart. Joshua scooped up the precious banner and, with flag in one hand and saber in the other, pressed forward. "Onward, boys! Onward!"

It struck like a lightning bolt. The minie ball tore into Joshua's right hip and exited the left leaving in its wake a severed artery, a nicked bladder, a serrated abdomen and a shattered pelvic bone.

Joshua fell among the dying. He expected death to visit at any moment. He could hear the rustle of her black taffeta dress.

"Stretcher bearer! We need a stretcher here!" Private O'Keefe knelt beside Joshua. "Don't move, Colonel. A stretcher is coming. I can see it now."

Joshua gazed at the panic-stricken boy he had sworn to protect. "Take heart," he whispered, lapsing into darkness.

Chapter 12

Joshua Is Gravely Wounded

Field surgeons led by doctor Shaw worked night and day to save Joshua's life. Shaw was the surgeon who had earned Joshua's admiration at Fredericksburg.

Joshua was hovering between life and death when an unexpected visitor arrived at the hospital ward and approached doctor Shaw.

"How is the Colonel?" asked the Commanding General of the Union Army, Ulysses S. Grant.

Shaw shook his head. "We've done all that we can, sir. It would take a miracle to save him."

Grant nodded, pained to hear the bad news. "May I see him?" It was an order.

"Of course, General." The doctor led the way to the private hospital room reserved for senior officers.

Grant stepped to the side of Joshua's bed. "I'm glad to see you alive, Colonel." He touched Joshua's shoulder. "I hear that you were gravely wounded gallantly leading your brigade into dangerous territory. In the face of the enemy you demonstrated outstanding valor above and beyond the call of duty. For your distinguished service, it gives me great pleasure to promote you to brigadier general."

Joshua could hardly speak. "Thank you, General," he whispered hoarsely, eyes welling with gratitude and pride.

It was the only battlefield promotion that Ulysses S. Grant ever bestowed. To many it was a death gift.

With the warmth of summer, Joshua barely clinging to life, was transported to the Naval Hospital at Annapolis. His tenacious will saw him through July and August. By September the miracle that surgeon Shaw had hoped for appeared, at last. Friends, family and fellow soldiers, who once visited with sad and hopeless eyes, now came more frequently with bright smiles and small gifts.

One day Tom came bursting into the room handing his brother a copy of the *New York Times*.

Joshua pushed up on an elbow. "What's all the fuss about, Tom?"

Tom grasped the newspaper thumbing through it until he found what he sought and returned the paper to Joshua.

"Good grief! I don't believe it! Whoever . . . ?" He had just read his own obituary. Beneath the modest headline was the printed report of Joshua's demise:

Colonel Joshua Lawrence Chamberlain was killed in action from wounds he sustained at Petersburg on June 13, 1864.

The brothers had their first good laugh in many months.

Joshua recovered at home for several more weeks deciding to rejoin his command even though he could not yet mount a horse or walk a great distance without assistance. Spurning all medical advice he returned to active duty in November 1864.

His recovery was a triumph of the human spirit inspired by his devotion to a noble cause: the preservation of the Federal Union and the abolition of slavery.

*　*　*

Joshua suffered agonizing pain from the wounds he sustained at Petersburg. From the time he rejoined his command until his death, pain was his constant companion.

By the icy winter of 1865, Grant ordered the final push. Brigadier General Joshua Lawrence Chamberlain, despite a stabbing pain in his belly, was determined to be a part of it.

At Quaker Road Joshua and his brigade engaged the enemy in hand to hand combat. He personally captured a squad of Rebels by convincing them that he was a Confederate officer after his uniform had turned gray with grit and smoke from the raging battle.

After securing the rebels as prisoners of war, he wheeled the faithful Charlemagne around and rejoined the battle in hot pursuit of the Confederate army.

Thwack!

A minie ball tore through Charlemagne's throat and lodged in Joshua's chest just below his heart. Charlemagne collapsed throwing Joshua head over heels onto the rough terrain, bathing both rider and steed in blood.

General Griffin, brigade commander, rushed to Joshua's aid. He bandaged rider and horse stemming the flow of blood.

Incredibly, a revived General and his steed rose up and rallied the brigade.

With Joshua looking like *pale death*, the battle reached fever pitch. Soldiers from both sides fell in droves. The battle raged with murderous fury with Joshua whipping his brigade forward. A final charge broke the back of rebel resistance paving the way for a Union victory.

General Horatio Sickel, himself badly wounded, observed a grief-stricken Joshua bowing his head for the fallen. "You have the heart of a lion, General, and the soul of a woman." With deep respect he saluted Joshua and placed his hand on his shoulder. "We should have more like you."

"Thank you, General. It was a hard fight." Joshua returned the salute. He scanned the battlefield looking for familiar faces. At that moment, a heavy downpour drenched them all – the living and the dead. "The heavens are weeping," murmured Joshua.

That night, as the rain pelted his tent, Joshua lit a few candles and prepared to write condolences to the families of boys for whom there would be no homecoming. One letter, above all, was the most painful. He sat, unmoving, before he could compel himself to write:

> My Dear Old Friend,
>
> It saddens me beyond measure to write and say that I could not keep my promise to you. Your precious son was killed in action at the Battle of Quaker Road on March 29, 1865. It grieves me to tell you that after all he endured, Divine Providence did not see fit for him to witness the final victory. I pray that you are able to take solace from the fact that he fought bravely and died honorably for our glorious cause.

Joshua's hands trembled. He wanted to say more. He would have to finish the letter another time. At sunrise a new battle awaited. For Private Ronald O'Keefe, not quite nineteen years from his birth, the battle had ended.

It was little comfort to Joshua that he received a promotion to Major General. He ignored his second obituary printed prominently in the *New York Times*.

Chapter 13

Victory!

The end of the war was in sight – the Confederacy's Waterloo. The Rebel army was collapsing and in full retreat in the aftermath of the Battle of Five Forks. Joshua led his brigade, now under the authority of General William Sheridan, in a race to crush the last remnants of Lee's army. The blazing assault carried them to the gates of Appomattox Station.

Sheridan ordered a final attack. Chamberlain commanded the infantry brigade. The cavalry was led by a new general, a rising star, bold and bright, barely twenty-six – George Armstrong Custer.

Joshua repelled one last desperate Rebel attack at White Oak Road. Ragged and suffering from starvation, Lee's army ground to a halt.

That evening, there was a disturbance outside Joshua's tent, a clamor of stomping boots and shrill whistles. He walked into a rowdy commotion. "What is it, Tom?"

"Lee wants to stop the fighting! He's requesting a pow wow with Grant about the terms of surrender."

The brothers embraced.

As word spread, the cheers and hurrahs shattered the chilly night air. Soldiers pummeled each other in ecstatic celebration. Victory songs rang through the camp. Grown men wept. The long awaited words for which they hoped and prayed all these hard fought years, heard at last. *Cease fire!*

Joshua breathed deeply. He had fought in twenty battles, had five horses shot from under him, been wounded six times and had read his obituary twice. He was truly a child of fortune.

Chapter 14

Surrender at Appomattox

General Chamberlain assembled his victorious brigade and they marched to the courthouse at Appomattox Station. The brigade in giddy anticipation waited, and waited. And waited. It was April 8, 1865, a milestone in the nation's life. A country reunited.

A white flag of truce fluttered in the breeze. Within minutes, coming from the south, a gray bearded man cantering on his famous horse, Traveler, approached the Appomattox Courthouse. Carrying himself with dignity, befitting a General, Robert E. Lee led a small cadre of southern cavalry. Joshua stared at the historic figure, committing his face to memory.

He turned to his brother. "We have defeated them, Tom. Now we must lead them home."

From the north, slumping in his saddle, leading a detachment of Union officers, supreme commander of the Union Army,

Ulysses Simpson Grant squinted into the bright April sky. His blue slouched hat was cordless and he wore an ordinary soldier's blouse, unbuttoned. His pants were tucked into mud-splashed high boots and while he looked like a common soldier, the four gold stars on his lapel said he was a man to be reckoned with.

Grant dismounted lightly. He strode past Joshua who, filled with awe, neglected to salute him.

Grant approached his enemy. The two deadly foes, under the white flag of truce, saluted each other. Ritual completed. Grant ushered Lee into the Appomattox Court House.

One of Lee's senior commanders, conducting himself with full military bearing, strode up to Joshua and saluted. "General Chamberlain, I am General James Longstreet."

Joshua recognized both the name and the man. He was one of the finest and bravest senior commanders of the Confederate Army. "General Longstreet." He snapped a crisp salute.

"I understand General Grant has ordered that all provisions be withheld from my men."

"Yes, General. That is the order."

"Sir, my boys are starving. They are broken and defeated. I'm requesting food and water for them. They have given their all and are in dire need."

Joshua met James Longstreet's eyes. Face to face with this proud and gallant man who was willing to humble himself for the good of his men, Joshua relented. "General I believe I can meet your request. I will give the order."

"Thank you, General. I'm at your service, sir."

Word spread like wildfire: "They're working out the terms of Lee's surrender!" "The war is over!" "It's really over!" "We can go home now. Lord, bless us. We can go home!"

*　　*　　*

"Any news, Tom?" Joshua was waiting for word of the official surrender of the vanquished Southern Army. A clatter of hoof beats approached the command post.

Tom raised the tent flap. "A courier from General Grant."

"See what he wants."

Tom slipped out of the tent and was surrounded by a growing buzz of voices.

Joshua continued writing a condolence letter to the widow of General Fred Winthrop. He remembered the exact moment of Winthrop's death as if he were gazing at a snapshot: *Five Forks. The last day of battle – he and Winthrop are sitting on camp chairs. They are eating a simple lunch, talking about the war and how it's progressing – about family and home. It is a rare moment of quiet and peace. Suddenly, in mid-sentence, Winthrop slumps over. A bullet has shattered his brain. The sniper is nowhere in sight.*

Tom stepped into the tent. "News about the official surrender."

"Let's have it, brother."

"April 12th. Appomattox."

"That's it? That's all the courier had to say?"

"No, there's more."

Joshua grew impatient. "Lieutenant!"

"Sir! General Grant has appointed an officer to accept the formal surrender of the Confederate Army."

"Who gets the honor?"

"Guess."

"Tom, you're already stretching my patience."

"Oh, if you must know."

Joshua knit his eyebrows and frowned deeply.

"It's you, Joshua!" It was the first time since the outbreak of the war that Tom saw his brother rattled.

"Me? Why me? I'm not regular army, not West Point. I'm only a citizen soldier. What a great honor! I'm astonished at Grant's choice."

"Astonished? Why *you*? Let me tell you why you. Grant was looking for an officer who was brave but not reckless. Loyal to the Cause *and* the truth. Bold but responsible. A crafty leader but obedient and prudent. Shall I go on?"

"No, no, no."

"Need I say that your Medal of Honor citation is for conspicuous gallantry and distinguished service."

Joshua was deeply touched. His eyes misted. "Enough," he said. "I yield."

General Ulysses S. Grant had looked for a man with simple dignity after so bloody a war. He had taken his Commander-in-Chief's good advice: *Let 'em up easy.* Lincoln's ardent hope was to bind the nation's wounds, *with malice towards none and charity for all.*

* * *

April 12, 1865. A chilly day, as gray as the broken Confederacy. Gray as the threadbare uniforms they wore. "This is more like April in Maine, not Virginia." Tom rubbed his hands together, fighting the impulse to shiver.

Joshua, in full dress uniform, waited at the rear of his brigade lined up on both sides of the dusty road leading to Appomattox Court House. At the order the gray ranks of the Stonewall brigade, led by General Gordon, marched two abreast between the Union troops. Chamberlain's boys braced at attention, spines straight, eyes facing the long gray columns.

As the Stonewall brigade arrived at the designated area to surrender their weapons and flags, Joshua gave a remarkable command to the bugler – a command that reflected the honor and compassion that was the hallmark of his life. The bugle sounded loud and clear. The Union infantry shifted their muskets from the routine "order arms" to "carry arms" which signified honor and respect.

General Gordon, the much admired commander chosen by Lee to carry out the surrender, sat a little taller in his saddle stunned by this gesture of honor. The generosity of saluting a fallen enemy touched him deeply.

Gordon returned the courtesy. He wheeled his horse around and rode up to Joshua. The great beast reared, his forelegs high in the air. When they again touched the ground the animal lowered its mighty head and executed a deep bow. Then with one sweeping movement, General Gordon unsheathed his battle sword and touched his boot toe with the point of his weapon. "Carry arms!" he ordered.

The Rebels obeyed their commander answering honor with honor. It was a stirring moment for both sides.

One by one, in silence, the Rebels stacked their arms and cartridge belts. They folded their tattered colors with reverence and stacked them atop each other.

Joshua's voice was firm. "General, I regret that I cannot allow you to keep your colors."

"I understand," Gordon replied. "You have been a shining knight in this bitter war."

Joshua with all modesty ignored the compliment. "General Grant has ordered that your troops may keep their horses and mules for the spring planting."

"You astonish us with your generosity."

Joshua's brigade was flushed with triumph. Gordon's cadre of officers were embittered. Still, Joshua was hopeful. "Brave men may become friends," he said.

He was met with stony silence. It was too soon.

Chapter 15

Touched by Fire

Triumph turned quickly to tragedy. Before the jubilant Union Army had time to savor their victory, a telegram arrived from Washington, DC with heart sinking news.

On Easter Sunday, 1865, as Joshua led his troops on a grueling march to Richmond, he caught sight of Tom galloping towards him at breakneck speed. Before the dust had settled, Tom dismounted his horse waving a piece of paper.

"What is it, Tom?" Panic twisted his belly.

"Telegram."

Joshua grabbed the telegram from Tom's trembling hand and unfolded the yellow sheet. He gasped. "Not Lincoln! Terrible news for the country, especially the South."

"How could this have happened? John Wilkes Booth, that sniveling actor!"

"He was a fanatic supporter of the Confederate cause. War makes good men better and bad men worse." Joshua could not answer Tom's unanswerable question.

"First the war, now this. It will never be the same."

Joshua tried to console his brother, but he could only mouth empty platitudes. "Great crises in human affairs call out the great in men."

Tom buried his head in his hands. "The South has lost its best friend and the country has been robbed of a great leader. Maybe, in time, I will find your words comforting. But not now, Joshua. Not now."

"I know, Tom. He is as much a casualty of war as any 'Billy Yank' from Bull Run to Five Forks. As Secretary of War Stanton said, 'Now he belongs to the ages.'"

*   *   *

The newspaper went wild. Photographs of the martyred President were seared into the memory of every soldier and civilian. The ill-fated rebellion had spawned the murder of the innocent on both sides of the battle.

A bizarre footnote claimed the life of Lieutenant George Wood, one of Joshua's junior officers from the original 20th Maine. On the night that Lieutenant Wood was wrongfully killed by one of his own men, a thunder storm assailed the brigade. A huge bolt of lightning split the torrential night reminding the weary troops of war's destruction.

Joshua's wartime journey had ended where it began. On May 23, 1865, the Union Army reconvened for the Grand Review in Washington, DC. Joshua, mounted on Charlemagne, led his brigade past the reviewing stand and the new president, Andrew Johnson.

As an honored guest General Joshua Lawrence Chamberlain joined the President and the other dignitaries on the reviewing stand. Joshua saw them all as they passed, the fine young men, living and dead, who had fought for a glorious cause . . . O'Rorke . . . Weed . . . Hazlett . . . Vincent . . . O'Keefe . . . Wood . . . and countless others who had sacrificed their lives. Joshua thought : *Surely the heavens must be draped in black bunting.*

The American Civil War claimed more lives than all wars in American history combined. More than one million men, women, and children perished or were maimed. Thousands were confined to insane asylums, their minds completely destroyed. Victims of what became known as "soldier's heart" never saw daylight again. One in ten northerners were killed or crippled. One in four southerners met the same fate.

Bowdoin – it was only four years ago, yet it seemed like eons. He recalled the words he shared with his students: "Sometimes war is a necessary evil, but even when necessary, it is always evil."

"What about a just cause?" a student had challenged.

"When the cause is just, the war is necessary," replied Joshua, "but the slaughter and brutality make it evil."

Joshua saw groups of children waving miniature flags as the parade marched by the reviewing stand. He heard their shouts of approval and excitement as he stood at attention. His generation had been touched by fire. Would this young generation be spared?

Abraham Lincoln,

*The Gettysburg
Address*

November 19, 1863

Four score and seven years ago our fathers brought forth, on this continent, a new nation, conceived in Liberty, and dedicated to the proposition that all men are created equal.

Now we are engaged in a great civil war, testing whether that nation, or any nation so conceived, and so dedicated, can long endure. We are met on a great battle-field of that war. We have come to dedicate a portion of that field, as a final resting-place for those who here gave their lives, that that nation might live. It is altogether fitting and proper that we should do this.

But, in a larger sense, we can not dedicate – we can not consecrate – we can not hallow – this ground. The brave men, living and dead, who struggled here, have consecrated it far above our poor power to add or detract. The world will little note, nor long remember what we say here, but it can never forget what they did here. It is for us the living, rather, to be dedicated here to the unfinished work which they who fought here have thus far so nobly advanced. It is rather for us to be here dedicated to the great task remaining before us – that from these honored dead we take increased devotion to that cause for which they here gave the last full measure of devotion – that we here highly resolve that these dead shall not have died in vain – that this nation, under God, shall have a new birth of freedom – and that government of the people, by the people, for the people, shall not perish from the earth.

Epilogue: Taps

In 1865, at age 37, Joshua retired from the army and went on to live a rich and adventurous life. His curiosity about the world and his passion for learning led him to acquire a personal library of more than two thousand books on subjects ranging from ancient languages to modern investing. He invested his money wisely in New Jersey Railroads and the New York Power Company. Then, attracted to the climate, he bought land in Ocala, Florida, which he sold at a large profit.

A year after the Civil War ended, he was elected Governor of Maine in a landslide. He served four terms, supporting capital punishment, fighting against the impeachment of Andrew Johnson, and campaigning for Ulysses S. Grant in 1868.

He was a founding member of the Army of the Potomac Association, the largest brotherhood of Civil War veterans.

Joshua returned to Bowdoin College and taught every subject with the exception of mathematics. Following his teaching career he was appointed president of Bowdoin where he modernized and broadened the course of study. Confronting strong opposition from zealous Calvinists, he added science to the curriculum, proclaiming, "I do not fear any man of science."

Always proud of the military, Joshua introduced military science to Bowdoin. He was forced to drop it from the curriculum when a student protest and boycott known as the *Drill Rebellion* was successful.

Most controversial of all – President Chamberlain raised tuition from $60 to $75 a year causing distress to both students and their parents!

He was the U.S. Commissioner for Education at the Paris Exposition.

During a period of great upheaval caused by economic unrest, political gangs resorted to violence and shook the state of Maine. Joshua's leadership quelled the riots and lifted the siege.

He went on to become president of *New England*, a popular magazine.

Joshua's admiration and lifelong love of the arts inspired the *Institute for Artists and Artisans* in New York City to elect him their president.

As a man of letters, he wrote numerous articles and authored several books.

In 1898, at age seventy, Joshua volunteered to fight in the Spanish-American War although he still suffered from wounds inflicted during the Civil War. To his great disappointment, he was rejected because of his advanced years.

He died on February 24, 1914 at the age of eighty-five, finally succumbing to the grievous wounds he suffered at Petersburg in 1864. He was the last Civil War veteran to die of his battle wounds. As his casket was lowered slowly into the earth the haunting bugle call, *Taps*, lingered in the icy Maine air.

Edwards Brothers Malloy
Thorofare, NJ USA
November 23, 2016